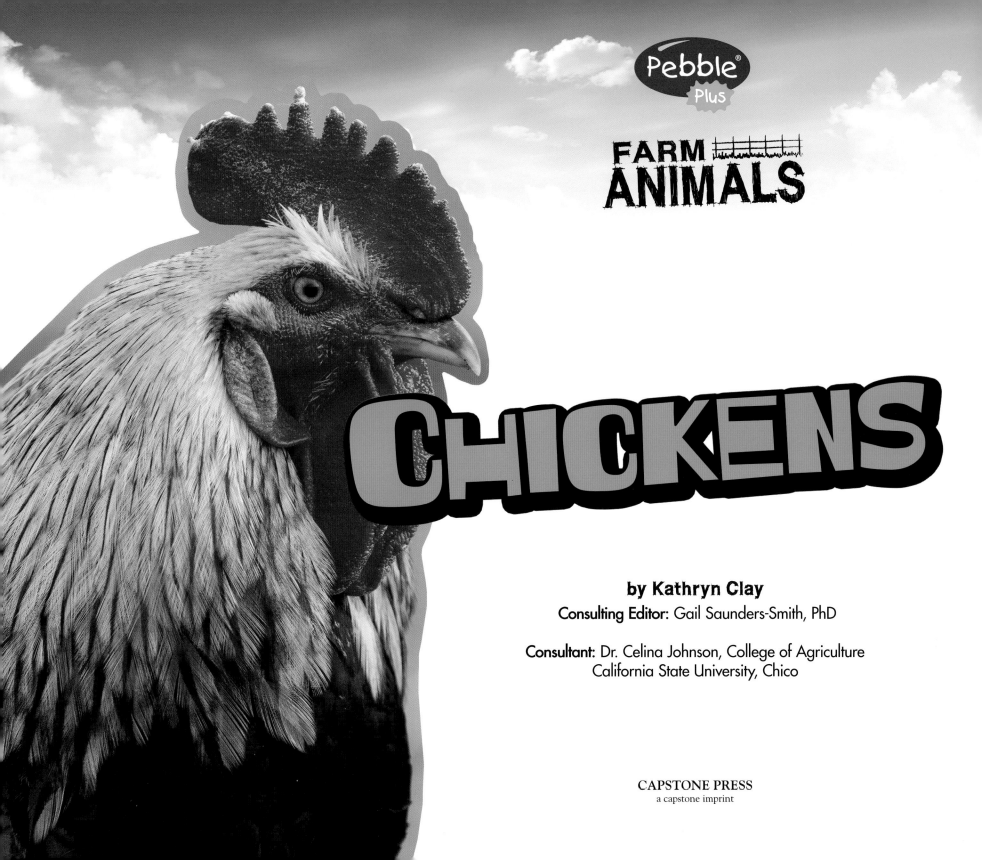

Pebble® Plus

FARM ANIMALS

CHICKENS

by Kathryn Clay

Consulting Editor: Gail Saunders-Smith, PhD

Consultant: Dr. Celina Johnson, College of Agriculture
California State University, Chico

CAPSTONE PRESS
a capstone imprint

Pebble Plus is published by Capstone Press,
1710 Roe Crest Drive, North Mankato, Minnesota 56003.
www.capstonepub.com

Library of Congress Cataloging-in-Publication Data
Clay, Kathryn.
Chickens / by Kathryn Clay.
p. cm.—(Pebble plus. Farm animals)
Includes bibliographical references and index.
Summary: "Simple text and full-color photographs provide a brief introduction to chickens"—Provided by publisher.
ISBN 978-1-4296-8650-1 (library binding)
ISBN 978-1-62065-298-5 (ebook PDF)
1. Chickens—Juvenile literature. I. Title.
SF487.5.C53 2013
636.5—dc23
2011049977

Editorial Credits
Erika L. Shores, editor; Ashlee Suker, designer; Marcie Spence, media researcher; Eric Manske, production specialist

Photo Credits
Alamy Images: D. Hurst, 17, Greg Wright, 21; iStockphoto: Lawrence Sawyer, 19; Shutterstock: Borko Ciric, 13, Groomee, 11, krugloff, 15, liubomir, 7, Lurii Konoval, cover, 1, tepic, 5, Tomas Sereda, 9

Note to Parents and Teachers

The Farm Animals series supports national science standards related to life science. This book describes and illustrates chickens. The images support early readers in understanding the text. The repetition of words and phrases helps early readers learn new words. This book also introduces early readers to subject-specific vocabulary words, which are defined in the Glossary section. Early readers may need assistance to read some words and to use the Table of Contents, Glossary, Read More, Internet Sites, and Index sections of the book.

Printed in the United States of America in North Mankato, Minnesota.
042012   006682CGF12

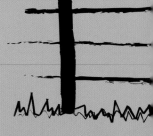

Table of Contents

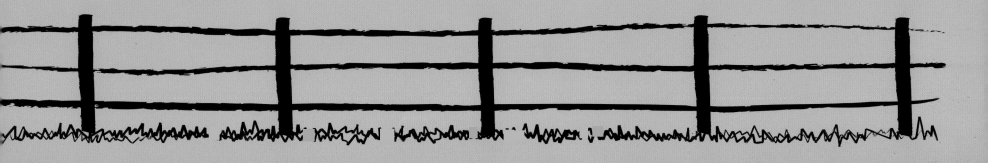

Meet the Chickens

Cock-a-doodle-doo!

A rooster crows as the sun rises.

Chickens dash around the farm.

Most chickens have white,

brown, black, or red feathers.

They peck with sharp beaks.

Below the beak of some chickens

is a red flap of skin called a wattle.

wattle

Chickens weigh about

7 pounds (3 kilograms).

Chickens can fly only short distances.

Their small wings cannot lift

their heavy bodies.

New Life

Male chickens are roosters.

Hens are female chickens.

Only hens lay eggs.

rooster

hen

Hens sit on eggs to keep them warm.

Crack! Eggs hatch after 21 days.

Young chickens are called chicks.

On the Farm

Chickens eat feed made

of corn, wheat, and seeds.

Chickens also scratch the ground

for insects and worms.

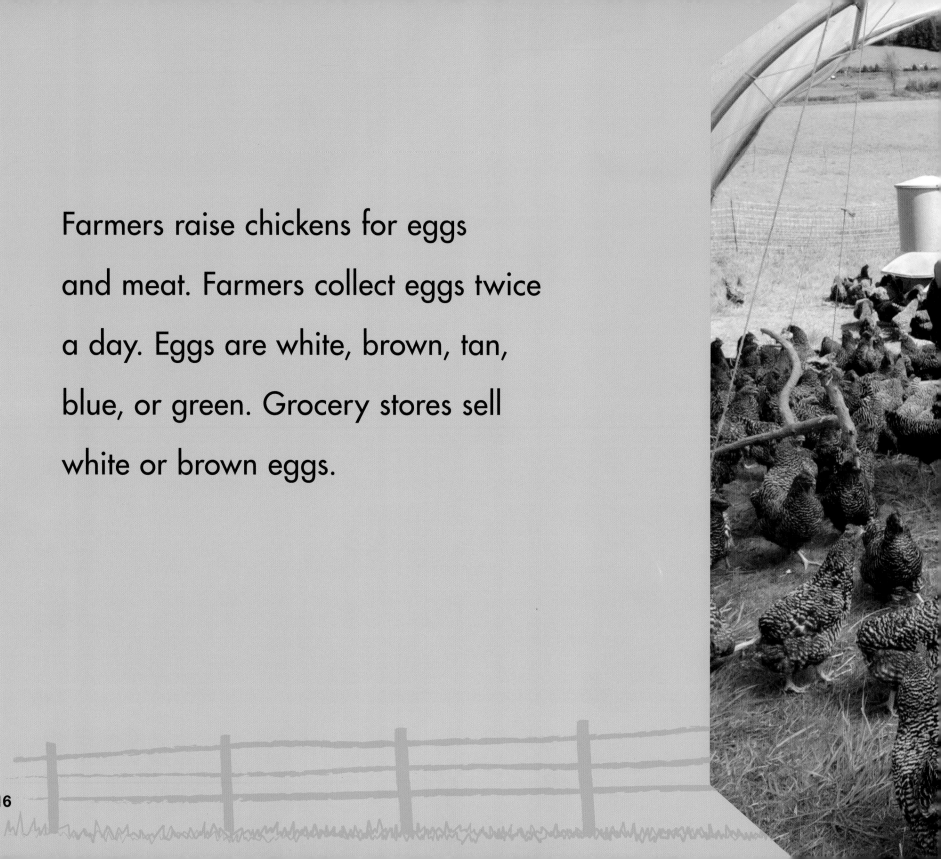

Farmers raise chickens for eggs and meat. Farmers collect eggs twice a day. Eggs are white, brown, tan, blue, or green. Grocery stores sell white or brown eggs.

Chickens are also kept as pets.

Some chickens let you hold them.

They may eat out of your hand.

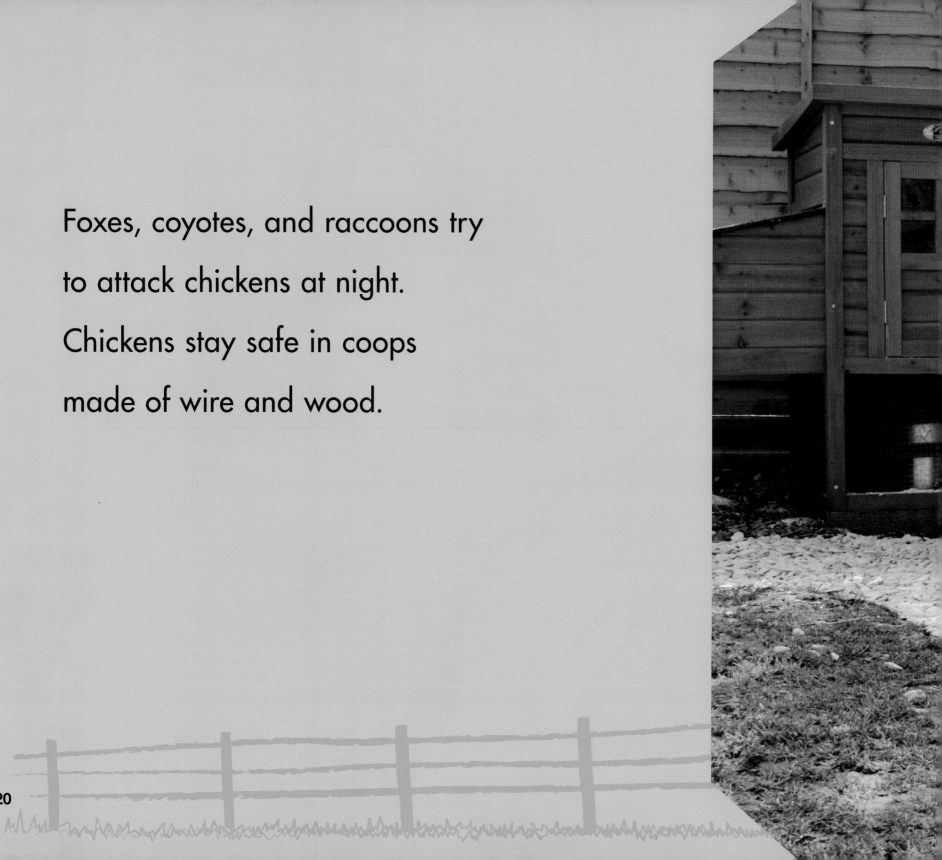

Foxes, coyotes, and raccoons try
to attack chickens at night.
Chickens stay safe in coops
made of wire and wood.

Glossary

beak—the hard front part of the mouths of birds

coop—a small building where chickens stay safe and lay eggs

dash—to move quickly and suddenly

hatch—to break out of a shell

hen—a female chicken

peck—to pick at something

rooster—a male adult chicken

wattle—a piece of skin that hangs down from the chin of some birds

Read More

Macken, JoAnn Early. *Chickens*. Animals That Live on the Farm. Pleasantville, NY: Weekly Reader, 2010.

Mercer, Abbie. *Chickens on a Farm*. Barnyard Animals. New York: PowerKids Press, 2010.

Nelson, Robin. *Chickens*. Farm Animals. Minneapolis: Lerner Publications, 2009.

Internet Sites

FactHound offers a safe, fun way to find Internet sites related to this book. All of the sites on FactHound have been researched by our staff.

Here's all you do:

Visit *www.facthound.com*

Type in this code: 9781429686501

Super-cool stuff! Check out projects, games and lots more at **www.capstonekids.com**

Index

Word Count: 179
Grade: 1
Early-Intervention Level: 14